THE INTERNATIONAL POCKETBOOK

CU00405937

By David Horchover
Revised and updated by Jim Sherlock and Mark Robson

Drawings by Phil Hailstone

"The trouble with today's business environment is that if you do not risk the opportunity to embrace exporting, you risk even more. This creative little guide will help your journey into a new and exciting world, removing many fears about exporting."
David Russell, Managing Director, D3Direct Limited, London Heathrow Airport.

CONTENTS

INTRODUCTION

INTRODUCTION

EXPORT FACTS AND FIGURES

- British firms trade in every market in the world

- Second largest exporter of services and fifth largest exporter of goods in the world. We export more than £4,000 a year for every man, woman and child in the UK

- The UK leads the world in several fields; pharmaceuticals, aerospace, the creative and entertainment world, finance and business services

- British companies earn a staggering £230 billion per year from selling their products and services overseas – more than the combined GDP of Denmark, Ireland and Portugal in 1999

The UK desperately needs to improve its export performance simply to maintain, let alone increase, its share of the world's fast-growing international trade. Current exporters need to research further new markets; those not exporting yet should be encouraged and helped to begin.

Properly undertaken, exporting can be both fun and profitable!

INTRODUCTION

WHY EXPORT?

- **Under-used capacity:**
  - exporting could allow you to increase production, reduce unit costs and increase profits

- **Diversity:**
  - some markets are more prosperous than the UK and have more disposable income, eg: the USA and some EU countries
  - a spread of markets helps to avoid slumps in one

- **Peaks and troughs:**
  - home market prone to seasonal activities
  - home market may be declining, but opportunities exist abroad or can be developed

Important: Always ask 'What if?' questions and write down the answers. Don't gloss over anything, and be totally honest with your answers.

DIFFERENCES

- Buyers are further away (usually)
- Contractual terms will have to be strictly honoured
- Longer credit periods are likely to arise
- Financing and cash flow problems could occur
- Political risks, customs regulations, documentation, customer credit-worthiness have to be addressed
- Foreign currency and exchange risks need to be understood
- Language and legal processes are different
- Transport systems/shipping arrangements need to be understood, even if you work with a freight forwarder

EXPORTING COMMITMENT
THREE KEY REQUIREMENTS

1 Management commitment to exporting

2 Products or services with genuine potential

3 Sufficient capacity - both production and management - to meet demands

These are the three key requirements for those who wish to develop a proper export operation which will produce the required return on investment in money, time and effort.

5

GETTING STARTED

DESK RESEARCH

WHAT TO LOOK FOR

Finding out about the market before taking the plunge and deciding to export is **worth the cost.** Regard it as an investment!

Main concerns should be:

- Background to the target market, eg: economics, politics, currency
- Market size and the likely product demand
- Competitive products - quality, prices and origin - already in the market
- Tariff or import restrictions, ie: duties, quotas, taxes on imported goods
- Distribution channels and methods, eg: agents, distributors, wholesalers, retailers
- Technical standards to be met

DESK RESEARCH
WHAT TO LOOK FOR

Other considerations will be:

- Location and number of customers/outlets

- Credit worthiness, credit terms and payment methods

- Packing and packaging for export (especially labelling regulations)

- Literature and support material (consider language problems/needs)

- Currency to be invoiced in, ie: sterling, local currency, or other, eg: Euro, US dollars

- Much of this information can be gathered from the internet or from your local Business Link

(9)

GETTING STARTED

FIELD RESEARCH

INTERNATIONAL MARKET RESEARCH

- Involves gathering information by means of interviews and questionnaires
- More expensive than desk research
- Complements and enhances desk research, especially if it is qualitative, undertaken to gauge potential customers' attitudes

Where possible, always conduct desk research and field research to give a more accurate picture of the intended market.

You will reduce the risk of failure and improve the chances of success.

Funding and training is available through the Export Market Research Scheme (02476 694492).

CHECKING COMPETITION

It is amazing, but true, that so many businesses with good products and ideas for business at home fail to take a hard look at the competition they are going to face abroad.

There are very few products that have a uniqueness which precludes competition, either directly or by substitution.

Competitors should be known almost as well as your own business.
'Know thine enemy'.

KEY ISSUES

- **ACCESSIBILITY**   Which markets offer the best potential; what is their position on tariffs, import duty or quotas?

- **PROFITABILITY**   What is the pricing level for your type of product - will it produce sufficient profit on sales?

- **MARKET SIZE**   Is the market currently big enough or will it grow to a size to be worthwhile?

OBTAINING INFORMATION

- Look within your own organisation, eg: staff, reports, documents, past sales
- Obtain competitors' catalogues and price lists; they can be most revealing
- Check trade directories, trade associations, trade journals, technical publications
- Use International Trade Teams in Business Links and Chambers of Commerce, foreign embassies for data, background information
- Consult specialist libraries, eg: Trade Partners UK Information Centre
- Watch out for special reports and surveys in the press (the Financial Times is an excellent source)
- Ask the international division of your bank
- Use the internet

OBTAINING INFORMATION
CAUTION

Be wary of data held or compiled abroad or taken from the internet. It can be seriously flawed, especially if it comes from an emerging or developing nation.

- It could be several years out of date
- Data may not be compatible between two countries because of lack of standardisation
- May be based on some tax-based function, eg: value-added tax or equivalent

Check

- What products were included in the product classification/grouping
- Who originally collected the data and why; was there any motive for misrepresentation
- How the data was collected and over what period
- Does the data link consistently with other local/international data

WHICH PRODUCTS?

FIRST QUESTIONS TO ASK

1 Can my firm's product be exported as it is?

Benefits
- Economies of scale
- No development or amendment costs
- No special components or technological contents required
- Minimisation of marketing costs
- Universal appeal, eg: jeans, Kodak film, CD's, Pepsi, Coca Cola

2 What mandatory changes could affect the product?

Examples
- Legal requirements, eg: minimum standards
- Tariffs
- Technical - voltage, measuring system
- Taxation policy in intended market
- Climate conditions in potential markets (some countries may require special composition)

(15)

PACKING CHECKLIST

First check:

- Climatic conditions to the destination country and in transit to point of purchase
- Handling of the product in transit - methods used and frequency of handling
- Time factors: how long the product will be in the distribution chain
- Consumer usage rate and the consequent storage time
- Package size - what is the most practical, convenient or price-sensitive size for the market

Then check:

- The cost of packaging
- Local preferences (in colours and illustrations on pack)
- Legal requirements, ie: what has to be shown on pack

LABELLING CHECKLIST

Exporters must adhere in every country to local regulations.
This is what is usually required:

- Manufacturer's name
- Country of origin
- Weight
- Description of contents
- Nature of ingredients

Note: This is not a detailed list of labelling requirements. Exporters are advised to seek advice from the Trade Partners UK website: www.tradepartners.gov.uk or from the Trade Partners UK Enquiry Service, tel: 020 7215 5444/5.

LABELLING
LANGUAGES

Regardless of government regulations, every manufacturer or exporter will require a label, at the very least, to communicate information to customers or users, to:

- Facilitate the product's use, construction
- Assist in customer satisfaction
- Encourage initial and repeat purchase

Advice: Labels should be written in the most appropriate language(s). For example, in Canada, French and English are required, unless the product's national image is particularly important, eg: Scotch whisky and French perfume.

- Multi-lingual labels/instructions for use in several countries will reduce costs but should only be used if this enhances a multi-national image; it is usually better to have local language labels, although more expensive

GETTING STARTED

SERVICING PRODUCTS OVERSEAS

If you have a product which may require servicing, you must have a proper servicing policy.

- Customer satisfaction and goodwill are paramount and need to be maintained

but

- Costs or investment must be carefully calculated - including training
- Organisation must be of the highest order

Options

- Set up your own servicing operation
- Appoint distributors to carry out the servicing

Tip: Consumer goods which do not need servicing will still require a customer-satisfaction policy, eg: money back/replacement scheme.

OPTIONS FOR SERVICING

Your own servicing organisation

- **Benefits**   Customers see that you are totally committed to their country and your product quality
- **Drawbacks**   Sheer cost of setting up and maintaining a service division; it may be more sensible to fly out trained staff for more expensive/capital equipment

Appointed Distributor

- **Benefits**   Speed, local knowledge, lower costs
- **Drawbacks**   Customers like to deal with company representatives. Also it requires locating a network which will work to your standards. The original exporter will need to watch their performance closely.

DELIVERING SERVICE PRODUCTS

Services need to be delivered in real time to people (such as legal services or training) or to things (such as renovation of machinery or buildings or much environmental consultancy). Many companies deliver services profitably overseas and the UK is the second largest exporter of services in the world.

In most cases a company will either need to send staff to work in the country to deliver the service or obtain staff based in the market. Locally based staff can be directly recruited, sub-contracted or provided through a joint venture agreement.

You may also need to consider what other facilities (such as office or workshop space) and equipment (such as fax and machinery) you will need.

Tip: In many countries the British Embassy can provide short-term facilities such as meeting rooms and, in some cases, temporary office space.

DELIVERING SERVICE PRODUCTS

You should ask yourself:

- Can the service be delivered remotely through the internet or other means?
- Can it be easily standardised and sub-contracted or licensed?
- Will the service content need to be changed for the target market?
- What risks are associated with employing or sending staff overseas?
- Who actually will travel overseas to deliver the service?
- What training will they need in languages and cultural skills?

Note: Be sure to identify any specific restrictions such as membership of professional bodies, health and safety legislation and employment law.

AGENTS AND DISTRIBUTORS

METHODS OF SELLING OVERSEAS
DIRECT SELLING

It is important to select the right route at the start.

Direct Selling: sales made direct from manufacturer/exporter to customers abroad without any kind of intermediary.

Ideal for	• Industrial/capital goods
	• Goods sold to national governments and other official bodies
	• Consumer goods via direct mail/mail order
	• Consumer goods sold direct to retail stores, particularly large store groups
Benefits	• Face to face selling produces excellent results
Drawbacks	• High cost of overseas representation

If selling direct is not suitable for you, you will need to consider some of the methods described on the following pages.

AGENTS AND DISTRIBUTORS

METHODS OF SELLING OVERSEAS
USING THE INTERNET

There are many myths about the use of the internet and IT to sell overseas. Whilst there are companies which have created new markets by the use of a website, there are also many websites which have not brought in one pound of new business.

A website needs to be known if it is to be used. You must:

- Market the website by including it in all literature, letters, etc
- Make sure it is registered regularly with the major search engines (you can buy cheap software which can do this)

A website needs to be fully integrated into your overall promotional strategy. It is not a stand alone activity.

Perhaps the most commonly successful area is in building and maintaining relations with existing clients.

UK Online for Business, based at your local Business Link can provide detailed advice and support in setting up an effective website.

AGENTS AND DISTRIBUTORS

METHODS OF SELLING OVERSEAS

USING THE INTERNET

There are five levels of use of the internet:

Level 1 - Messaging: exchange of messages through e-mail.

Level 2 - Publishing: use of a website as a shop window.

Level 3 - Interacting: using a website to provide an electronic catalogue so that people looking at the site can see your product range. It may include the ability to order online by filling in an order form online. Payment will be by existing off line methods.

Level 4 - Transacting: a transactional website covers the whole process including ordering and payment for a product.

Level 5 - Integrating: this means the full integration of ICT into a business so that, for example, stock levels are recorded online and automatic reordering takes place when they get below a certain level.

You will need to think about which is appropriate for you and your clients.

AGENTS AND DISTRIBUTORS

METHODS OF SELLING OVERSEAS

EXPORT MERCHANTS

Domestic wholesalers operating in foreign markets through their own salesforce, agents, stockists and, often, local branch offices. Their remuneration is the difference between buying and selling prices.

Export Houses usually specialise in product groups or territories.

Benefits for you	● Local knowledge of market
	● No need for you to finance the exports
	● No paperwork or documentation to worry about
	● No credit risks
	● No executive overheads
Drawbacks	● Exporter has no control over the market
	● Exporter builds little or no goodwill
	● Exporter's products may receive little attention from the export house

METHODS OF SELLING OVERSEAS

CONFIRMING HOUSES

- **Confirming Houses**

A Confirming House acts as a principal for an order placed by a foreign buyer in the UK with a manufacturer who is unwilling to extend credit overseas. That is, it finances the transaction, accepts the short term credit risk and receives a commission from the buyer.

- **Buying/Indent House**

A Buying House acts on behalf of an overseas buyer, either buying with discretion against orders received or placing indents on manufacturers specified by the buyer. It may act as a principal like the Confirming House.

- **Manufacturers' Export Agent**

This type of agent sells overseas on behalf of UK manufacturers, sometimes in its own name, but more usually in the name of the manufacturer, covering a specific sector of business.

Benefits and Drawbacks

Similar to those of trading through an export merchant, except:

- The manufacturer, selling in his own name, retains greater control over market
- Exporter is responsible for finance, credit risk and all documentation

METHODS OF SELLING OVERSEAS

SPECIALIST EXPORT MANAGER

● Specialist Export Manager

The Specialist Export Manager offers a complete export management package. In effect, they become the export 'department' acting in the manufacturer's name. They will usually undertake finance and handle all documentation, even accepting credit risk on occasion.

The manager makes their remuneration by way of commission on sales. Sometimes they may be paid an annual retainer.

Benefits	● Low cost 'export department'
	● Maximum degree of control over the market
	● Build-up of goodwill in company's own name
	● Long-term relationship
Drawbacks	● The export manager may try to pick better sellers
	● When sales develop the manufacturer wishing to go it alone will lack experience
	● Many export managers will expect a world-wide brief without having the skills or facilities to handle such a brief

(29)

AGENTS AND DISTRIBUTORS

METHODS OF SELLING OVERSEAS

- **International Trading Company**

These are highly diversified and large-scale manufacturers and merchants operating at both wholesale and retail levels. For UK exporters, dealing with a UK trading company is broadly akin to dealing with a UK merchant house.

- **Piggy-Back Exporting**

This system operates when one manufacturer (the 'carrier') uses their established overseas distribution facilities to market the goods of another manufacturer.

The carrier either sells the rider's product on a commission basis or buys them outright and acts as a merchant.

Benefits
- Rider - simple low-cost method of breaking into new market
- Carrier - fills gaps in own range, producing economies of scale in distribution

AGENTS AND DISTRIBUTORS

METHODS OF SELLING OVERSEAS

- **Export Consortia**
Where a number of exporters combine to tender
or bid for a major contract which singly they
could not hope to win

- **Buying Offices**
Many major international
department stores maintain
buying offices in the UK; they
may buy direct or appoint UK
export houses as their agents

Check carefully whether any
of these methods could
work for your company.

AGENTS AND DISTRIBUTORS

AGENCY

If none of these systems meets your requirements, you should look at the possibility of appointing an agent or distributor.

What is an Agency?

- The legal relationship which exists when one person or company (the agent) is employed by another person or company (the principal) to bring that principal into a contractual relationship with third parties

- A sales agent is employed to bring about a sales contract between his/her principal and a third party, the customer

- An agent (or the agency) never takes title to (or owns) the goods; title in them passes, as the result of the agent's efforts, directly from principal to customer

- The agent or agency receives a commission by way of remuneration

- An agent is not therefore 'employed' in the sense that he/she is on the payroll of the principal

4 TYPES OF AGENT

There are four main types of overseas agent:

Commission Agent
The most common form, with the agent (selling via samples or catalogue) merely passing orders direct to the principal who delivers to the customer; many industrial goods are sold this way.

Agency with spares and service facilities
Similarly an agency may carry stocks of spares, and provide servicing and repair facilities for which it charges the customer, usually at a scale of charges agreed with the principal.

Del Credere Agent
More of a contractual arrangement which could apply to any form of agency; the agent accepts any credit risk on behalf of his/her principal, paying the principal if any customer defaults.

Stocking Agent
He/she actually holds stock of the principal's products, providing storage and handling facilities, but still does not take title to the goods. A stocking agent will be paid a commission on sales and a fixed sum to cover storage and handling.

OVERSEAS AGENTS

Agencies can be:

- Individuals
- Partnerships, or even
- Small companies specialising in representation

They can also be:

- Large scale merchants
- Trading houses
- Manufacturers wishing to exploit their established overseas distribution system

BENEFITS OF AGENTS

- Exporters gain the services of an experienced local national who knows the local business customs
- An agent may have complementary products and contacts which will make market entry easier and quicker
- The investment cost is nil or negligible
- Exporters gain valuable market experience and can test sales potential
- Results (sales) can be immediate

DRAWBACKS OF AGENTS

- Too many lines carried

- As sales develop, it may be better to open your own branch office

- If the market has real potential the agent may not be able to exploit it

- Lack of commitment to your company/product

- Short term view - if sales do not arrive quickly, agents lose interest

DISTRIBUTORS

What is a distributor?

Distributors are customers who have been granted exclusive or preferential rights to purchase on their own account and re-sell a specific range of products or services in specified geographical areas or markets.

Distributors are wholesalers who make their 'remuneration' from the difference between their buying and selling prices.

4 TYPES OF DISTRIBUTOR

There are four main types of distributor:

- **Sole**   Where a sole distributor is appointed no other distributor will be appointed in that territory; the manufacturer can, however, exercise their right to sell in that territory

- **Exclusive**   Where even the manufacturer is de-barred - unless the agreement permits otherwise - from selling the contracted goods; nor may they appoint another distributor in the territory

- **Non-exclusive**   A manufacturer would be permitted to sell directly into the territory **and** also appoint other distributors in that territory

- **Selective**   This form of distributorship is used when the goods are of hi-tech standard or quality, sold via approved dealers who have staff with specialist skills or training, eg: computers, cameras, scientific equipment, etc

AGENTS AND DISTRIBUTORS

AGENT'S DUTIES

What are an agent's duties?

An agent must:

- Communicate all information to his or her principal and comply with reasonable instructions
- Act dutifully and in good faith
- Look after his/her principal's interest
- Make proper efforts to negotiate such business as is entrusted by his/her principal

These points are covered under E.C. Directive 86/653 (Directive on the Co-ordination of the Law of Member States relating to self-employed commercial agents).

AGENTS AND DISTRIBUTORS

PRINCIPAL'S DUTIES

What are a principal's duties?

- Provide to the agent all documentation and information necessary for the performance of the agency agreement
- Inform the agent of his or her acceptance, refusal or any non-execution of the business the agent has arranged
- Notify the agent as soon as it is anticipated that the volume of business will be considerably lower than the agent could have possibly anticipated

Important: Directive 86/653 specifies a minimum time within which notice to terminate an agency agreement should be given: 1 month in year 1; 2 months in year 2; 3 months in subsequent years.

AGENTS AND DISTRIBUTORS

SEARCH AND SELECTION

First check

Is an agent the channel most appropriate to your organisation?
If 'yes' - then:

Draw up an Agency Profile

You need to establish:

- The precise territory the agent **already** covers
- The type of customers or distribution channels to which the agent is **already** selling
- The completeness and frequency of the agent's sales coverage
- The types of products ideal as complementary lines
- Any requirements in terms of servicing, repair or stockholding facilities

Many of these points covering agency search, selection and agreements are common to both agents and distributors **BUT** legal advice should always be sought.

AGENTS AND DISTRIBUTORS

SEARCH AND SELECTION

WHERE TO FIND HELP

FLOOR	
1	**Trade Partners UK**
2	**Chambers of Commerce**
3	**Banks**
4	**Trade Associations**
5	**Agents' Associations**
6	**Advertising in relevant trade journals**

42

AGENTS AND DISTRIBUTORS

SEARCH AND SELECTION
FIRST STEPS

First - visit the market. This is essential.

- Make sure that the person who goes is in a position of authority and will be either immediately or ultimately responsible for the subsequent results

Then - check:

- Agency executives, sales people and other relevant staff, eg: service engineers
- Customers and prospects, ie: the companies to which the agent will be selling your products

AGENTS AND DISTRIBUTORS

SEARCH AND SELECTION
CHECKLIST

Then make a Checklist:

- Who owns the agency
- Career histories of executives
- Other agencies held and success record
- Areas regularly covered
- Types of outlets covered
- Frequency of calling

- Number of sales people, their length of service and qualifications
- Agent's true knowledge of the market
- Agent's marketing competence
- Bank and Trade references
- Agent's interest in and enthusiasm for new products, and yours in particular

AGENTS AND DISTRIBUTORS

AGENCY AGREEMENT

What should be included? The most common features are:

- Parties; who are they and can they contract
- Purpose of the agreement; what is to be done, sold, etc, and who is to do it
- Products; definition of products subject to agreement - now and in the future
- Territory; where the agent is entitled to act
- Exclusivity; who else may sell (or not) in the territory
- Duties of the agent and principal
- Commission; how paid, on what and when

AGENTS AND DISTRIBUTORS

AGENCY AGREEMENT (Contd)

- Performance targets
- Duration of the agreement
- Termination; this is possibly the most important clause and it must clearly state how and when a contract can be terminated
- Arbitration; in the event of disagreement
- Assignment; the agent cannot assign the benefit of the contract
- Authentic text; if the text is in two languages, which text is authentic
- Law of agreement; which national law governs the contract

Always seek professional advice!

AGENCY MOTIVATION

You want to ensure that your products receive a fair share of the agent's attention - preferably more! Here's how this can be achieved:

- Visit regularly; this shows interest and commitment to the agent and the market

- Work closely with the agent to show him/her how to profit from your product(s)

- Demonstrate where possible new outlets or opportunities exist

- Help prepare marketing and sales plans for the agent

(47)

AGENTS AND DISTRIBUTORS

AGENCY MOTIVATION

- Communicate; **both** ways - get formal reports regularly; exchange essential information, eg: prices, terms, personnel, new products, etc

- Keep informal, personal matters and information flowing - it helps consolidate a good agency relationship

Finally - if any difficulties arise with the agent, **interpret the agreement in the agent's favour.** Goodwill is worth more than the commission paid in marginal cases.

AGENTS AND DISTRIBUTORS

PARTNERSHIP & CONTRACTUAL DEALS

One approach is to enter into an arrangement with a partner abroad. These can be either a licensing agreement, a franchise or a joint venture.

- **Licensing**   Covers a wide range of agreements relating to the sale or leasing of industrial or commercial expertise in return for an agreed form of remuneration, paid on a regular basis.

- **Franchising**   Is a form of licensing most suitable for products which are not patentable; franchising is a fast-growing system of marketing worldwide.

- **Joint venture** A company owned jointly between two or more companies. This is an increasingly common feature of the business world.

Licensing and franchising both have benefits and drawbacks. It is particularly important to have professional advice before entering into any form of licensing/franchise agreement.

LICENSING
BENEFITS

Benefits of Licensing

- Market access - licensing permits entry into markets which could be closed because of high duties, tariffs, quotas, prohibitions, etc, high freight charges or entrenched competition

- Little capital investment is required and should produce a higher return on capital employed

- Penalties for failure are low

- New products can be quickly exploited

- Local partner can create new market using existing contacts

LICENSING

DRAWBACKS

Drawbacks of Licensing

- Competition from licensee when the contract expires
- The fees received may not compare favourably with a company's own manufacturing operation
- Quality control may be difficult to maintain from a distance

Points to check

- Take care selecting a licensee
- Make sure you have some degree of control
- Make sure you keep the licensee well motivated

AGENTS AND DISTRIBUTORS

FRANCHISING
BENEFITS AND DRAWBACKS

Benefits

- Franchising is a hugely popular method of developing a business concept in other countries and it is well worth considering as a system of marketing abroad

- With a great degree of control resulting from the supply of ingredients, franchising offers the possibility of revenue from a product that is not patentable

- Other benefits are similar to a licensing operation

Drawbacks

- Franchising requires many outlets (usually) and the search for competent franchisees can be expensive and time-consuming

AGENTS AND DISTRIBUTORS

JOINT VENTURES
BENEFITS & DRAWBACKS

Benefits

- Unlike other arrangements, you have total control as owner of the company
- Often, by sharing information and expertise, you get access to new ideas and products
- Funding is often easier to obtain
- You have a presence in a market
- In some countries this is really the only entry method

Drawbacks

- JVs require investment and, therefore, financial risk
- If not careful, it can go horribly wrong

AGENTS AND DISTRIBUTORS

JOINT VENTURES

KEY ISSUES

Care needs to be taken to find the right partner for a joint venture. There needs to be a mutual benefit to the arrangement and a clear strategy for the joint company.

Potential problems can arise because:

- During development of the JV, no one checks whether all parties have the same understanding about what has been agreed
- Cultural differences and misunderstandings
- Different management styles and business practices
- Legal constraints
- Drift in objectives

Note:

- This is a complex area and specialist legal and business advice should be sought
- There are various funds available to identify JV partners. Contact your Business Link for information

PRICING

PRICING FOR EXPORT

THREE OPTIONS

There are basically only three approaches exporters can adopt.

1 **Competition-oriented pricing:** mainly found in commodity markets (tea, wheat, sugar) where prices tend to move in unison.
2 **Cost-oriented pricing:** a company quotes a price based on its total costs plus a percentage for profit. Used mainly in the selling of industrial goods.
3 **Demand-oriented pricing:** requires an assessment of the intensity of demand. Price-setting becomes flexible. Used mainly in the mass consumer market.

Points to consider:

- Profit maximisation in the long run
- Market penetration - low prices to gain/capture market share
- Market skimming, ie: high prices at launch
- Early cash-recovery to generate cash flow

Pricing correctly is vital, and is an area which causes most initial problems.

THE EXPORT EQUATION

Exports attract costs not incurred in the home market. Many can therefore be overlooked in the export equation. Here is a brief checklist:

Start with the ex-works price
- The direct cost of manufacture plus export costs (paperwork, packing, etc) and profit margin

Add in distribution
- If F.O.B. (Free on Board), include transport and insurance to ship/airport and handling charges
- If C.I.F. (Cost, insurance, freight), also include transport to country of destination and insurance in transit
- If local market price, also include landing charges, internal transport, mark-ups and various taxes and duties

Promotion
- **Leave nothing out.** Think about agency commissions, exhibition charges, translation expenses, printing, product servicing, even product labelling

Sundry
- Could include cost of credit, credit risk insurance, forward exchange cover, import certificates, consular invoice fees

INCOTERMS

Never confuse the method of calculating costs and pricing with **INCOTERMS.** These are standard terms used globally to indicate the basis of delivery of goods. The booklet 'INCOTERMS 2000' from Chambers of Commerce is recommended.

The most commonly used terms are:

FOB	Free on Board		**CPT**	Carriage Paid to
EXW	Ex Works		**DAF**	Delivered at Frontier
CFR	Cost and Freight		**DES**	Delivered ex Ship
CIF	Cost, Insurance and Freight		**DEQ**	Delivered ex Quay
CIP	Carriage and Insurance Paid to		**DDU**	Delivered Duty Unpaid
FCA	Free Carrier		**DDP**	Delivered Duty Paid
FAS	Free Alongside Ship			

Advice:

- Quote as the customer/buyer requests and add the extra cost as required by the term of delivery
- If the customer/buyer does not specify then you select the term - usually FOB. For EU countries this should be DDP.

WHICH CURRENCY?

Is it better to invoice in your own currency or your customer's?

Sterling
- Administratively simple for the **exporter**
- The risk of exchange rate fluctuation is borne by the importer/buyer

Foreign Currency
- Administratively simple for the **importer**
- Foreign currency invoicing can lead to finance abroad at a better rate
- Quoting in foreign currency may help win the business
- Forward exchange cover may mean extra profit when the account is settled - this is a form of insurance which helps minimise risks of receiving less than the invoiced amount upon conversion to sterling

BARTER OR OFFSET

Barter   ●   There are some transactions which are termed 'barter or offset deals'. This is the direct exchange of goods for goods. Barter deals can be very profitable but new exporters should seek professional help before becoming involved

Some advantages:

- offers access to some markets which may otherwise remain closed
- barter contracts may be bigger than could be generated through 'cash' transactions

Advice: -   try to get at least part payment in cash

        -   make sure in advance that you can dispose of the barter goods

        -   check for UK import restrictions on barter products

        -   add in bartering costs to export contract price (especially agency fees)

MARKETING

MARKETING

OVERSEAS PROMOTION

Exporters will always have to persuade users and buyers to demand their goods in preference to any others. Here is a guide to the most effective methods.

Personal selling - always the best method

- Know your products, terms, prices, delivery, etc, absolutely, so that you can complete deals on the spot
- Appreciate local buying systems and cultures
- Plan and cost your visits carefully
- Set yourself clear objectives

OVERSEAS VISITORS TO UK

- Encourage buyers to visit your company
    - it creates goodwill
    - is less expensive than overseas travel
    - allows buyers to meet staff they will be dealing with

- Get involved with Trade Partners UK supported Inward Missions and Meet the Buyer events

- Use the visits to generate publicity wherever possible

63

MARKETING

PUBLIC RELATIONS

There are many ways to get coverage in the media, both here and overseas.

- Central Office of Information (the Government's main publicity body) will help with overseas publicity, featuring stories, products, photos in foreign media
- BBC World Service promotes new British products and ideas
- Send details of your export successes to your International Trade Team at Business Link or Chamber of Commerce for use here and abroad
- Trade Partners UK publish case studies
- Invite foreign reporters to visit

MARKETING

TRADE FAIRS/EXHIBITIONS

Far more important overseas than in UK.

Advantages
- You can see many prospects at once (reducing time and travel cost)
- You can demonstrate/show your product
- May be the only way to meet the end-purchaser

Help Available
- UK Government provides financial support to companies participating in overseas exhibitions (a list of those supported can be found on www.tradepartners.gov.uk – choose your 'sector' and then pick 'events')

MARKETING

TRADE FAIRS/EXHIBITIONS

Points to consider in deciding whether or not to attend:

- **Your objectives**
  - taking orders on the stand
  - taking enquiries for later follow-up
  - general market publicity
  - assessing/meeting agents and distributors
  - conducting low level market research

- **Type of exhibition**
  - general trade fair or specialised (industry) exhibition
  - national or international exhibition
  - open to trade only - or public also
  - special event, or permanent, eg: British Export Marketing Centre in Tokyo

STORE PROMOTIONS

These are often arranged by Trade Partners UK who provide funds towards promotion expenses **for the store** - not to participating British companies.

Benefits
- Can assist in long-term marketing planning
- Will help products already in the store

The long-term value of store promotions is difficult to assess but for many consumer/edible products they can be a low-cost, high-return activity.

MARKETING

SALES LITERATURE

Tips
- Use what you already have (leaflets, catalogues, instructions) but consider what adaptations may be necessary

- For translation work, use a translation agency familiar with your product or industry

- Check the sense of the translation by having it put back into English

- If using English text, keep it simple; avoid wordplay and humour

- Check colours, and use of people in illustrations, for suitability

MARKETING

SALES LITERATURE

Tips • Design literature for home and overseas use at the same time, thinking of

   - pagination, eg: Arab languages run
     right to left and from back to front

   - layout, eg: Chinese copy
     runs vertically; German takes
     25 % more space

• Build up your own mailing lists
   where possible; they will be
   more accurate (and cost you
   less to mail) than those
   from other sources

MARKETING

ADVERTISING

If you decide it is really necessary:

- Do not let your local agent/distributor handle it
- Do not join in shared advertising

It is almost always a failure.

If you want to advertise, control the budget and media yourself.

Tips
- Use your customers when choosing media - get them to recommend which are best
- You can use your domestic agency to book space in overseas media
- Take care what you say in the copy; no point in advertising 'labour-saving' in countries where labour is cheap

GIFTS AND SAMPLES

- These are usually asked for or offered
- They do build goodwill so it makes good sense to provide items related to your product or company
- Make sure gifts, etc, carry your company name, logo or brand name
- Limit distribution to customers, good prospects
- Watch the costs carefully and limit the use of samples to specific events
- Minimise 'avoidable' waste
- Think about who the gifts are targeted at. Get something appropriate

71

SALES PROMOTION BUDGETS

- Relate the amount of revenue you hope to gain from export sales to the amount of money that has to be spent to obtain that revenue

- Allow in your costs x% for promotion costs and arrive at the figure from past sales or from anticipated sales

- Forecast what it will cost you to obtain a certain revenue from a specific part of the world; decide if it will be worthwhile

Advice:
- Monitor all promotion costs against results, regularly
- Allocate expenditure to nominated territories
- Don't spend all the budget if you don't need to

This one area can cause exporters considerable difficulty and concern. It deserves a great deal of attention, not only to what you are trying to achieve, but to the amount that you can realistically afford from your overall budget.

TRANSPORT

FACTORS TO CONSIDER

If you have been asked to arrange shipment, you decide the method of transport. (If not, then you must follow your buyer's instructions.)

Advice: Always check carefully which method of transport is most suitable, considering:

- Speed
- Cost
- Security
- Safety
- Efficiency

The wrong choice could affect your bottom line.

TRANSPORT

BY SEA

- Sea is the cheapest system but slow, with the extra risks of damage, loss or pilferage
- Exporters can deliver to a container depot rather than a sea port
- Roll-on/Roll-off ferries allow exporters to use road and rail transport in tandem with sea transport in one operation
- 'Conference Line' ships run regular services at set rates
- Tramp ships run whenever there is a cargo, at negotiated rates

TRANSPORT

BY SEA

RATES

- Conference lines operate fixed tariffs; if you always ship this way, claim at least 10 per cent discount

- Non-conference ships - you pay less but have to bargain and you will not know the sailing date

- Sea freight rates are based on weight or measurement, whichever is the higher, which means you must weigh the goods in kgs and measure them in cms and cube the result

- Shipping lines work on the basis that 1 cu metre equals 1 metric tonne (1000 kgs)

- Rates will vary according to destination and type of goods; there is a minimum rate

- Freight is usually payable in advance and quoted in US dollars

TRANSPORT

BY AIR

Air freight is becoming more common.

- It's quick
- Less packing is required
- Less chance of damage or loss/pilfering
- Small quantities mean less money is tied up in stock in transit

However:

- It is costly
- It is limited to items able to fit on aircraft
- Possibly prone to delay through poor weather, mechanical problems

TRANSPORT

BY AIR

RATES

- Rates are fixed by IATA (International Air Transport Association)

- There is little difference between the rates charged by the airlines

- Reduced rates can be obtained through freight forwarders, who can negotiate with airlines to offer consolidation and other services

- The ratio used (since weight is more 'valuable' than size) in calculation is 6,000 cubic centimetres to 1 kg, ie: cargo is charged by weight rather than volume

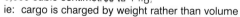

BY RAIL

- The Channel Tunnel now makes shipping to Europe more efficient
- Rail is quicker than road
- There is a sophisticated network of cargo trains operating throughout Europe
- Rail is usually the most reliable system, less subject to delays than air or sea

Drawback: Rail is not door-to-door

BY ROAD

- Door-to-door service
- Few delays across European frontiers now
- Useful for smaller exporters because of the 'groupage' system, ie: consolidation of a number of exporters' shipments
- Lower costs than air shipment and not always much slower
- Regular services to main cities are maintained
- Channel Tunnel has reduced transit times

BY ROAD AND RAIL

RATES

- Road rates are extremely competitive
- Rates for rail are standard, although major, regular shippers can negotiate
- Destination and type of goods carried will determine the rail route
- Road and rail both use the same ratio used for sea transport

PARCEL POST

This is an excellent service offered by the Post Office to countries all over the world.

Benefits

- For speedy service of certain items Datapost is excellent; items are simply handed in over the counter
- For regular exporters a door-to-door contract service is available

Limitations

- Items have to be acceptable by letter/parcel post
- Contents are subject to customs regulations in destination country
- Size limits apply
- Maximum weight is 15 kg, except to Japan and Malaysia - 10 kg

Full details available from Post Offices.

TRANSPORT

COURIER COMPANIES

There are now a number of private carrier companies which specialise in:

- Personal deliveries
- Office to office deliveries
- Airport to airport deliveries

Items handled

- Samples
- Spare parts/accessories
- Artwork for ad agencies, printers, etc
- Computer tapes
- Films
- Medicines
- Small items of equipment and consignments where speed is vital, plus security

Some courier companies, eg: TNT, DHL, offer worldwide services with their own transport. Each operates its own size and weight restrictions.

83

PACKING AND MARKING

PACKING

If you have no experience in packing for export, consult an export packing company or freight forwarder. Consider the following:

- Liability to damage or loss
- Type of transport being used (eg: sea will require more packing than air, rail more than road)
- Compliance with local customs regulations
- Climatic conditions in transit and in the country of destination (extremes of temperature and damp)
- 'Dangerous Goods' will need special packing and labelling
- Carrying of fragile goods will require special packing/labelling - which way up and where hooks (if any) may be used
- Resale value of packing materials

PACKING AND MARKING

MARKING

- Whichever transport system you use you must mark the consignment with the consignee's name and address
- Do not indicate the contents, to prevent theft
- By sea, only use order number, destination, name or mark of the consignee, the number of packages in the consignment and the number of each, eg: No 3 of 15
- Put the metric weight and measurement of each package on each parcel

Tip: When shipping goods include a packing list in the documents and keep a detailed list with all relevant packing and marking data.

BASIC DOCUMENTS REQUIRED
BY SEA

- Begin with the **'booking form'**, either a standard shipping instruction or a line's own

- Next is the **'Standard Shipping Note'** (SSN) which must accompany goods sent to the dock or depot before loading and shipment can take place

- The next item is the **'Bill of Lading'** which acts as proof that the goods have been loaded and are in good order (or not); this document is most important because it also acts as a contract of carriage and as title to the goods - **the goods will only be released to the person holding the original bill**

Note: A Sea Waybill is merely a variation of a Bill of Lading but it is not a document of title. Bills of Lading come in sets with so many originals and so many copies.

TRANSPORT

BASIC DOCUMENTS REQUIRED
BY AIR

- The airline, or more commonly a freight forwarder, will make out an 'air waybill' and send you your copy; other copies go to the consignee and carrier

- Air waybills do **not** act as documents of title but as contracts of carriage and for the receipt of the goods

- Airports store goods according to their air waybill numbers and all you need do is to advise your customer of this number for them to take the goods on arrival (subject to customs clearance where necessary)

BASIC DOCUMENTS REQUIRED

BY ROAD, RAIL, PARCEL POST

The basic documents are:

- CMR (for road) Convention de Marchandises per Routes
- CIM (for rail) Convention Internationale de Marchandises par Chemin de Fer

These act as:

- Receipt for the goods
- Contract of carriage

They do not act as documents of title as the goods will be delivered to the customer on arrival.

Parcel Post

- You will be given a receipt from the Post Office; this is a contract of carriage
- You may withhold delivery by asking the local postal service to collect payment before effecting the delivery
- The receipt is therefore not a document of title

DOCUMENTS REQUIRED BY IMPORTER

These are commercial invoices, movement papers and consular documents, required by the importer, and also by Customs for clearance and payment. Check your documents against the buyer's instructions, method of payment, and insurance cover.

Customs worldwide apply two types of barriers to imports:

- **Tariff** - duty, tax, excise, levy, licensing, quotas
- **Non-tariff** - technical, health and safety

Many importers have to seek permission before importing goods, for reasons of quota or foreign funds, which may be in short supply and strictly rationed.

Advice: Check with your importer in advance:
- Which documents are required before shipping (proof of the business)
- Do Customs require special documents with shipping paperwork?
- On what basis any duty is to be paid, by whom and when.

Get your paperwork right! Failure to comply with local regulations could lead to delays, fines or even the goods being impounded.

Information is available from your local Chamber of Commerce, Business Links or from the offices of Overseas Chambers of Commerce in the UK (London based).

89

TRANSPORT

CUSTOMS PRACTICE

- Customs worldwide control imports and exports
- You will be involved with Customs when goods leave this country and when they arrive in the destination country
- Exporters can obtain up to date information from their local H.M. Customs and Excise offices regarding the documentation they require
- The most important thing to remember is that, no matter who prepared the documents, **accuracy** is of **paramount importance**
- Exporters are **finally responsible** for the contents and accuracy of the information provided; wrong or false data could lead to legal proceedings

Advice: Seek advice from the start. Work with a freight forwarder.

TRANSPORT

FREIGHT FORWARDERS

Benefits of using a freight forwarder:

- Tells you of special requirements regarding the marking of your cargo and packing (some even pack for exporters)
- Advises you about customs requirements overseas
- Tells you the best shipping methods and routes
- Books space on your behalf and pays for it - most freight is paid in advance
- Makes out all documentation, eg: standard shipping note, customs entries, etc
- Declares goods on your behalf to customs
- Handles insurance on your behalf, if requested

A good freight forwarder removes the burden of paperwork. However, you are responsible for the accuracy of all data provided.

Contact BIFA (address at end of book) for list of names.

GETTING PAID

INVOICES

In international trade, invoices are used basically as a record of goods shipped and the terms on which they have been shipped.

- A 'Proforma' invoice is no more than an invoice used for making quotations with 'Pro-forma' written on it

- Where payment is made in advance, a 'pro-forma' is used as a means of getting payment from the importer/buyer

- Invoices are used for customs purposes; certified invoices or consular invoices are needed in many countries - Chambers of Commerce will advise you how they are processed for acceptance

- The exporter must prepare the invoice; a freight forwarder cannot - accuracy and honesty are vital

CASH IN ADVANCE

- This is the best system; with new customers it is also the safest!

- Payment is made against a commercial or pro-forma invoice; you clear the cheque and despatch the goods

- Payment can now be made quickly and securely by using computerised systems, eg: SWIFT (Society for World Wide Interbank Financial Telecommunications) - details from your own bank

LETTERS OF CREDIT

A documentary letter of credit (L/C) is simply an undertaking in writing by a bank to pay the exporter for his/her goods provided that he/she complies with the conditions laid down in the credit.

- Only about 20 per cent of world trade is conducted this way; however, there is a high rejection rate (over 60 per cent) because of errors or omissions
    - make sure they are properly completed
    - seek advice if in doubt as delay in payment could seriously hinder your cash flow and harm profits
- L/Cs protect the interests of both buyer and seller
- L/Cs ensure exporters get paid for their goods; importers don't pay until they receive documents which comply with pre-arranged conditions
- L/Cs specify when payment is to be made - usually when the documents are presented to the paying bank
- Be aware of how your bank treats L/Cs regarding funds/overdraft facilities and scale of charges

LETTER OF CREDIT

MAIN TYPES

- **Revocable**   Which means that the terms can be varied or cancelled at any time up to payment - **AVOID THEM**

- **Irrevocable**   Terms and obligations cannot be altered without all party agreement (NB all letters of credit are considered to be irrevocable unless specifically declared revocable)

- **Unconfirmed**   The seller is dependent upon the buyer's bank paying on time

- **Confirmed**   It guarantees payment irrespective of what may happen to the buyer's bank

  This is the most secure form of credit; if it is also **irrevocable** then this is even more secure

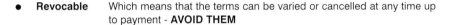

BILL OF EXCHANGE

- This is a demand for payment

- It is a written order by the exporter to their buyer, payable on demand - either payable **on sight** at a fixed future date or at **term** which is at a determinable future date, eg: x days after the date of an invoice

- The exporter's bank handles the paperwork/documents involved with the buyer's bank

Procedure:
- Draw the bill of exchange on your buyer; send it with relevant documents to your bank for 'collection'

- Bank sends papers to buyer's bank, who notifies buyer of their arrival

- Buyer's bank releases documents to buyer - who then takes delivery of the goods

- Payment should then be made to you/your bank

Caution: Credit is being given so only use a Bill of Exchange with reliable customers.

OPEN ACCOUNT

- When you know an overseas customer well, you may agree to accept payment on an agreed basis, eg: 30 days from the date of invoice
- It is the least secure method of payment but the most common; it can also be the least expensive, but check the cost with your bank
- Specify how you wish to be paid, eg: SWIFT, cheque or foreign draft
- Allow up to 7 days for your account to be credited
- Monitor the arrival of the funds, if your bank doesn't advise you
- Make sure all documentation is 100 per cent accurate - **always**; do not give the importer any reason for delaying payment

FACTORING

This is the term used when you 'sell' your debtor receivables, the management of collection being undertaken by a 'factor'.

Advantages

The factor:
- Checks the importer's credit rating
- Collects the money
- Generally guarantees 100 per cent to the exporter on an agreed date even if the importer has not paid the factor
- Saves an enormous amount of clerical work
- Eliminates foreign exchange risks
- Allows exporter to work on open account terms
- Allows exporter to finance overseas trade
- Often provides shipping and forwarding services
- Charges around $2\,^1/_2$ - $3\,^1/_2$ per cent of the invoiced amount

FORFAITING & INVOICE DISCOUNTING

Forfaiting

Some exporters selling capital goods are required to give long-term credit.

- 'Forfaiting' allows exporters to 'sell' the total amount they are owed for a discount
- Exporters are then paid that discounted amount with no further financial worries
- The forfaiter collects the money over the period of the contract

Forfaiting and factoring are somewhat akin to one another with forfaiting based on a larger scale.

Invoice Discounting

- This is similar to factoring but it costs you less as the discounting house does not become involved with collection
- It provides finance for an agreed period, usually to the end of the agreed credit period

COUNTER PURCHASE, COMPENSATION, SWITCH TRADING

Counter Purchase

- This is more common than barter trading; an exporter is asked to buy goods from the importer in exchange for goods he has supplied - amounting to the value of goods exported

Compensation (or buy-back)

- Where technical know-how, plus some equipment, is supplied by an exporter who then guarantees to 'buy back' the finished product to the value of the know how/technology supplied

Switch Trade

- Where an exporter is paid by a third party

Advice: All these schemes (Counter Purchases) can be very profitable. Contact a factor who can arrange such deals on your behalf.

GETTING PAID

CHECKING CREDIT

A good customer is one who pays regularly and on time. **Always check the credit worthiness of new customers.**

- Get the name and address of the buyer's bank
- Make a 'status enquiry' on the buyer's bank through your bank
- Always enquire for an amount **more** than the order value
- Never rush to deliver goods before enquiries are completed
- Ensure that the new customer is of good business standing and has a good record of payment
- Use a credit rating agency to get a full run down on the importer's business, eg: Dun & Bradstreet, High Wycombe
- When you are satisfied on all counts you can begin to trade

CONTROLLING CREDIT

- Devise a control system for controlling credit and age of debt, ie: length of time an account is outstanding

- Make checks regularly - this could be an 'early warning' system

- Review and update information regularly - allow more or less credit, longer or shorter periods, as necessary

Advice:
- One week before payment or settlement is due call the buyer to check that there will be no problems or delays

- Sales and Accounts departments should work closely together so that no more orders are taken from long-overdue customers (unless for very good reasons)

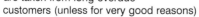

GETTING PAID

RAISING FINANCE FOR EXPORT

- **Bank Overdraft or Loan** — Backed with credit insurance (see page 107), exporters will stand a better chance of being granted facilities, as insurance provides security

- **Confirmed and Irrevocable Letter of Credit** — Exporters will have no need for insurance as the Letter of Credit will be sufficient security

- **Term Bill of Exchange** — This may be discounted and cash obtained from a discount house

- **Factoring and Forfaiting** — Already discussed - allowing cash to be received quickly

- **Confirming Houses** — Exporters are paid in sterling when goods are supplied

- **Bank Schemes** — Always check to see what special schemes banks may offer exporters to finance business

Advice: Talk to your bank before taking any final decision.

GETTING PAID

INSURANCE

GUARDING AGAINST FAILURE

An exporter has three options regarding risks:

- Insure against it in full
- Insure against it in part and bear the remaining risks personally
- Bear the whole risk, acting as self-insurer

Advice: Insurance should always be taken out to avoid unacceptably severe financial losses.

INSURANCE

3 GROUPS OF RISK

There are three groups of risk:

- **Commercial** Which means loss or damage to the cargo through specifically nominated clauses/reasons
- **Political** Which covers activities of governments
- **Credit** Which covers the inability (or unwillingness) of your customer to pay

Note: If you have to make a claim, make it as quickly as possible after the event and provide all documents.

MISCELLANY

PRE-SHIPMENT INSPECTION (PSI)

Some governments overseas insist on checking exports prior to shipment. Agencies are employed to check:

- The accuracy of documents
- Discrepancies (quality/quantity) in the goods or prices

These are the most important reasons.

Advice:
- Always comply
- Make sure all documents are available
- Check who will pay to restore the packing, post-inspection
- Appeal in writing in the UK and the importing country if there are concerns

A full list of countries using P.S.I. and their agents is available through your local Business Link or Chamber of Commerce.

EXPORT CONTROLS

Certain goods are subject to export control and approval **before** their export is essential.

Reasons:
- Security (UK & NATO)
- Foreign policy
- International treaty obligations
- Terrorism/repression in some countries

Advice:
- Always have a named person responsible for compliance in your company
- Always have a written procedure
- Always maintain records

Information regarding export controls is available from 'Export Control Organisation' of the D.T.I. who will advise on how to apply for certain licences.

Warning: Severe penalties are imposed for failure to comply with the system.
Most goods do not require an export licence but some may need an import licence for the country of destination.

MISCELLANY

PERFORMANCE BONDS

- If your business is involved in tendering or bidding for a contract, it may be necessary to submit evidence that you are serious and can perform the contract

- 'Earnest' money is a percentage of the tender price paid to the buyer to show your worth and intention

- Bid (or tender) Bond is a legal document issued by the tenderer's bankers which reflects the standing of the supplier

- Once the contract is awarded a Performance Guarantee or Bond replaces the Bid or Tender Bond

Advice:
- Always consult the bank if asked to put up a guarantee

- Only bid when you can deliver or fulfil the contract

- Always arrange a 'facility' with the bank

- Get confirmation of the cancellation/expiry of any Bond issued

112

CUSTOMS DATA

The information required by H.M. Customs and Excise need not be daunting.

- Check with your local Customs and Excise Office if in doubt or help is needed
- All goods exported from the UK have to be identified by a Commodity Code to be shown on all customs/transit documents (primarily to compile trade statistics)
- INTRASTAT collects trade data moved within the EU (not services)
- For goods sent outside the EU and to countries which have preference trade agreements with the EU, EUR 1 Customs form is required

Advice:
- Get details from H.M. Customs and Excise
- Freight forwarders will know what requirements have to be met

MISCELLANY

VAT AND EXPORTS

- On sales to buyers in countries outside the UK, invoices can be zero-rated, ie: UK VAT is not chargeable. Sales to the EU need the buyer's VAT registration number on the invoice.

Note:
- Sales to private buyers in EU countries, UK VAT is chargeable
- All VAT registered businesses must complete two relevant boxes on their VAT returns showing the value of supplies to and from EU countries
- Exporters are required to keep proper records to ensure all VAT and INTRASTAT statistics are correctly maintained

If in doubt, check with your local VAT office for full and up-to-date information.

MISCELLANY

INTELLECTUAL PROPERTY
TRADE MARKS/BRAND NAMES

- A Trade Mark identifies the origin of a product
- It assures the buyer/user of its quality
- It allows the manufacturer to promote his/her products without benefiting the competition
- Registration of a Trade Mark or brand name will give protection against misuse or misrepresentation, eg: passing-off and piracy
- Shapes and smells can now be registered in the UK

Check:
- Present and future market potential
- Ease and total cost of registration
- Costs of policing infringements and taking legal action
- The importance of having one standard international brand name

INTELLECTUAL PROPERTY
PATENTS, DESIGN AND COPYRIGHT

- Patent Protection - up to 20 years is available for a new product, material or technical process
- Registered Design - up to 25 years' protection for designs which must demonstrate aesthetic appeal
- Copyright - protection lasts 50 years after the author's death (with discussions currently underway regarding a longer period of 70 years); any original written work by authors, publishers and by authors of computer software programmes can be protected
- Unregistered Design Rights - owners can obtain protection for 5 years and for the following 5 years the owner can claim royalties for UK sales

Advice:
- Get help from a **Patent Agent**
- Contact the Patent Office in Newport, Gwent (01633 814000)
- Regard any costs as insurance
- Proper protection could ensure success overseas

MISCELLANY

LANGUAGE ABILITY

Why it is important

- Handling incoming phone calls from abroad is easier
- Quick translations of correspondence will give a good idea of its contents
- Buyers appreciate your effort and politeness in speaking their language
- Creates a good image and excellent PR if you can meet and greet overseas visitors in their own language - even if only a few words

Remember: Although English is regarded as the world's commercial language, and many have English as a second language, it should never be taken for granted that buyers will have any knowledge or command of English.

Important: You can speak all the languages you like, but if a caller can't get past the switchboard it's useless! **Train the switchboard.**

LANGUAGE TRAINING

Check your needs

- What do you really need to learn or acquire?
- To what level is training required?
- How much time is to be allocated to training/learning per week?
- Who in the organisation really requires tuition?
- Which training methods are best for the business - videos, disc, classroom?
- What is the cost? (usually between £20-£50 per hour)

Note:
- Proficiency for most western European languages can be reached in weeks
- Non-latin based and Far Eastern languages, allow 12-24 months

Contacts
- Languages National Training Organisation (020 7379 5131)
- LEXUS   Languages In Export (02476 694554)
- Local Business Link or Chamber of Commerce (0345 567765)

OPPORTUNITIES

Trade Partners UK is the Government's international trade development support organisation. Trade Partners UK has staff in most of the major cities in the world and throughout the UK.

A wide range of support is available from advice on starting to trade overseas to detailed advice about local culture and business practice by local staff. Detailed research can be carried out on a company's behalf, visits and exhibiting at trade fairs overseas can be subsidised, amongst a wide range of other opportunities and initiatives.

Trade Partners UK employ experienced business people as International Trade Advisers; they are based at and contacted through your local Business Link.

WHERE TO GO FOR EXPORT HELP

- Trade Partners UK (www.tradepartners.gov.uk)
- Banks
- Chambers of Commerce (www.britishchambers.org.uk)
- The Institute of Export (membership body) (www.export.org.uk)
- Overseas Chambers of Commerce
- European Commission Offices
- Foreign Embassies and High Commissioners
- Business Link
- Trade Journals and Associations

Advice:
- Use the business or reference section of a good library for initial information, phone numbers, addresses, etc
- Then prepare a more detailed outline of the information required before you call or visit any other organisation

USEFUL ADDRESSES

Trade Partners UK
66-74 Victoria Street, London SW1 6SW

Tel: 020 7215 5000
Fax: 020 7215 8266
Web: www.tradepartners.gov.uk

Institute of Export (Membership body)
64 Clifton Street, London EC2A 4HB

Tel: 01733 404400
Fax: 01733 404444
Web: www.export.org.uk

Customs & Excise
Head Office, H.M. Customs & Excise Dept,
New Kings Beam House, 22 Upper Ground, London SE1 9PJ

Tel: 0800 595000
Web: www.hmce.gov.uk

Chambers of Commerce
Coventry office:

Tel: 020 7565 2000
Tel: 02476 694484
Fax: 02476 695844
Web: www.britishchambers.org.uk

Business Link (For local contact)

Tel: 0345 567765

USEFUL ADDRESSES

SITPRO Ltd (The Simpler Trade Procedures Board)
Oxford House, 8th Floor, 76 Oxford Street, London W1D 1BS

Tel: 020 7467 7280
Fax: 020 7467 7295
Web: www.sitpro.org.uk
E-mail: info@sitpro.org.uk

Major Credit Risk Insurers

E.C.G.D. *(medium to long term cover, ie: 2 years plus)*
P O Box 2200, 2 Exchange Tower,
Harbour Exchange Square, London E14 9GS

Tel: 020 7512 7887

N.C.M. *(formerly E.C.G.D.)*
short term cover, ie: up to 2 years
Offices throughout the UK.
London address: N.C.M. City of London, 5th Floor,
63 Queen Victoria Street, London EC4N 4UA

Tel: 0800 2121310

Freight Information and Forwarders

British International Freight Association (BIFA)
Redfern House, Browells Lane, Feltham Middlesex, TW13 7EP

Tel: 020 8844 2266

USEFUL WEB ADDRESSES

1. **Trade Partners UK**
   Identify schemes and services provided by DTI and FCO Gateway site to a range of services for exporters.
   www.tradepartners.gov.uk

2. **Embassies (British & Foreign)**
   Both those based in UK and country of interest. www.embassyworld.com

3. **Local, Bilateral and Overseas Chambers**
   Local Chambers www.britishchambers.org.uk
   Bilateral and Overseas Chambers
   www.worldchambers.com

4. **International Organisations such as**
   NATO www.nato.int
   United Nations www.un.org
   Europa www.europa.eu.int
   International Trade Centre www.intracen.org/
   World Trade Organisation www.wto.org
   International Monetary Fund www.imf.org

5. **Cultural Aspects / Country Profiles**
   Doing Business in ... (CBI etc) www.cbi.org.uk
   www.tradeport.org/ts/countries/index.html
   www.americanexpress.com/homepage/smallbusiness.shtml (select Expanding Internationally)

USEFUL WEB ADDRESSES

1. **Industry / Sector Reports**
   Market Branches, Embassies, sector experts.
   www.tradeport.org/ts/industries/index.html
   www.corporateinformation.com www.eiu.com
   www.businessmonitor.com

2. **Local and Overseas Trade Associations**
   Contact your trade association, or others in a
   related field. www.martex.co.uk/taf/lookup for
   UK trade associations
   info.asaenet.org/gateway/OnlineAssocSlist.ht
   ml list some American and a few international
   trade associations

3. **Trade Literature & Journals**
   www.publist.com for on-line search.

4. **Newspapers & Press Clippings**
   www.thepaperboy.com links to over 4,500
   newspapers from 170 countries
   WWW.ONLINENEWSPAPERS.COM links to a
   similar number View the global archive at
   www.ft.com

5. **Trade Shows and Exhibitions**
   British Trade International supported events on
   www.tradepartners.gov.uk/gateway/live/events
   home.ds
   The Trade Show News Network www.tsnn.com
   Expo guide www.expoguide.com
   Trade Show central www.tscentral.com

6. **Leads and Information**
   www.theexportsite.com www.tradeuk.com

FACTS AND FIGURES

1. **Libraries**
   One of the best is run by Trade Partners UK, based in London and is worth a special visit. www.tradepartners.gov.uk/informationcentre, Universities, Business Links and local Chambers of Commerce may also have useful libraries, as may other bodies such as the Chartered Institute of Marketing www.cim.co.uk.

2. **Statistics Providers**
   Links to the statistical agencies of around 60 countries and international organisations. stats.bls.gov/oreother.htm

3. **Directories & Databases**
   Kompass www.kompass.com, Dun & Bradstreet www.dnb.com, Kelly's www.kellys.reedinfo.co.uk, Hoover's www.hoovers.com, Thomas Register (USA) www.thomasregister.com, Telephone books and Yellow Pages - select your country at www.wayp.com/ or www.mrweb.co.uk/dotcom/framecou.htm.

4. **Published Market Research**
   Not free, but often worth investment.
   Market Search www.marketsearch-dir.com,
   Findex www.marketresearch.com,
   Euromonitor www.euromonitor.com,
   Frost & Sullivan www.frost.com,
   Mintel www.mintel.co.uk.
   For a completely tailored approach to your market and industry, you may wish to consider using the expertise of the market research industry.

Market Research Consultancies
To search for those with experience in the industry and country: www.mrweb.co.uk/big, (for those based in the UK) www.bmra.org.uk, use selectline to find the right agency www.esomar.nl/index.htm, (for those based abroad or in the UK).

Source: BCCI Export Market Research Scheme 'Surfing Without Drowning'

About the Author

David Horchover MCIM

David Horchover MCIM is Principal of Chase International Marketing, an organisation he set up in 1990.

David Horchover worked for a number of major organisations before becoming International Marketing Director of a US-based sales and marketing company where he helped it grow into a multi-million pound operation with sales in most parts of the world. The experience gained over 15 years in a fiercely competitive environment proved invaluable, giving him a practical and hands-on knowledge of all aspects of export marketing and selling.

Horchover later became Sales and Marketing Director of the Institute of Export. He now writes regularly on export matters for a number of leading publications (he is Export Editor of Sales & Marketing Management) and lectures both in the UK and overseas on a wide range of sales and marketing-related topics. He also acts as a consultant to a number of clients. A Member of the Chartered Institute of Marketing for well over 30 years, David Horchover is a holder of the rarely presented Institute's President's Award.

First published in 1996 by:
Management Pocketbooks Ltd, Laurel House, Station Approach, Alresford, Hants SO24 9JH, U.K.
Tel: +44(0) 1962 735573 Fax: +44(0) 1962 733637 E-mail sales@pocketbook.co.uk
All rights reserved. Revised reprint 2001. Printed in England. ISBN 1 870471 99 7